SHOW LOVE NOW

By

SITERRA WALLACE-WALKER, M.S.W.

Copyright © 2021

ISBN: 978-0-578-83807-6

All rights reserved.

No part of this book may be reproduced, stored in a retrieval system, or transmitted in any form or by any means, electronic, mechanical, photocopying, recording, scanning, or otherwise, without the prior written permission of the publisher.

Disclaimer

All Biblical verses are italicized and taken from the New King James Version of the Holy Bible.

Every material contained in this book is provided for educational and informational purposes only.

No responsibility can be taken for any results or outcomes resulting from the use of this material.

TABLE OF CONTENTS

DEDICATION 5

ACKNOWLEDGEMENTS 7

INTRODUCTION 8

CHAPTER ONE: SELF-LOVE 10

CHAPTER TWO: ACTIVE LISTENING 17

CHAPTER THREE: SICKNESS 22

CHAPTER FOUR: DEPRESSION/SUICIDE 27

CHAPTER FIVE: MY DREAM GUY 33

CHAPTER SIX: COURTSHIP-WEDDING-MARRIAGE 40

CHAPTER SEVEN: ANNIVERSARIES 49

CHAPTER EIGHT: EMPLOYMENT 53

CHAPTER NINE: FUNERALS 60

CHAPTER TEN: BIRTHDAYS	65
CHAPTER ELEVEN: THINKING OF YOU	71
CONCLUSION	77
NOTES	78
ABOUT THE AUTHOR	83

DEDICATION

To my loving Father God, Jesus, His Son, and the Precious Holy Spirit, I thank you for the grace and direction to write this book. I affectionately dedicate this book to my dream come true, my Bishop, Senior Pastor, and best friend. To my loving, patient, and supportive husband, I thank you for enduring with me through this process. My love for you, Gregory Walker, shall live forever! To the members who are my cheerleaders at Life Kingdom Outreach Center, Inc., Apostles Emmanuel and Cheryl Williams, and the Imitators of God Ministries Family, I love you all. I want to especially thank my dear brother and loving sister who blessed me with three amazing nephews and a precious niece and niece whom I love immensely. To the awesome Wallaces and Gates extended family members, I love you all to life! To my loving auntie, Apostle Janice Dillard, and the entire Walker family, much love and hugs to you all. Finally, I am thankful for my prayer partner, Torrii and Loretta my two long-lasting friends; and my additional supportive friends who are literally like blood family to me (you all know who you are.) Much love to each of you!

ACKNOWLEDGEMENTS

I want to acknowledge Andrea Jackson, a warm, caring, and professional person, as well as the entire team at I.O.M. Publishing. Barbara Joe Williams, for the many years of encouragement, teaching, and getting me started on this book. Jasmine Underwood, for her tireless edits, words, and actions of support. Deborah P. Jackson, for listening to me and accepting me "as is" for 42 years! Jeffrey Lamar for letting me rent his talents. Many blessings to you all!

INTRODUCTION

Oh, the state in which we have found ourselves. Many in the world are searching for validation, searching for authentic relationships, and searching for intimacy in those relationships. In hindsight, the world is screaming for love.

Show Love Now is a compilation of experiences where the writer recognized reasons, scenarios, and often critical times to show love now. The book explicitly demonstrates when and how to communicate your feelings of love and gratitude in diverse situations. The thought of losing a loved one without a proper goodbye or visiting a loved one for the last time without expressing the sentiments of one's heart can be devastating. Frequently we may have these feelings or thoughts about a particular person. It is then that we should follow through with a "response" to those feelings or thoughts. People are here today and gone tomorrow.

The purpose of *Show Love Now* is to educate, cultivate, and motivate the reader to become more aware of individuals in their space and to actively reach out to them. There is an intentional call to action. Suggestions for reaching out in non-traditional ways are offered after each chapter. The reader is encouraged to literally jot down the person's name that comes to mind when reading the vignettes. Love is an action word, and "show love now" is an action-driven activity.

Enjoy your time as you go through the experiences and resolutions while you journey through *Show Love Now*.

CHAPTER ONE

SELF-LOVE

"To love oneself is the beginning of a lifelong romance."
~Oscar Wilde

Wow, self-love! Now, this is a thought-provoking, exciting, yet hands-on chapter to compose. Showing love to myself has always been challenging. There were several traumatic experiences throughout my life that invoked low self-esteem. As a direct result, self-care was never a priority for me. Self-care can include daily hygiene, regular exercise, healthy eating, spiritual fitness, positive affirmations, and healthy interpersonal relationships just to begin.

While writing *Show Love Now*, the daily struggle of overcoming the ability to "Show Love Now" to myself was very much a journey. One morning at 3 am, after a warm shower, I woke up to write this portion of the chapter. Since then, I have struggled with bouts of depressive episodes; there were continuous days of sleeping. Days lacking hygiene activities, days of eating little to no food, or often overindulging in food as it became a coping mechanism. As a side note, the excessive food intake took me to a disturbingly soaring weight of 394 pounds. The many combinations of days and weeks of inappropriate hygiene resulted in 13 teeth being extracted.

Not one of these facts was easily recognizable from an onlooker, co-worker, or casual friend. Why not, one might ask? I mastered the art of masking all the pertinent spots during my birdbaths. I then followed up maintaining with deodorant and lotion wherever it was noticeably required. I learned a behavioral modification technique from an awesome therapist. She suggested that I put out seven days of outfits and push through enough to make it to my appointments, job, or other expected religious/social gatherings. After I completed the activity, I would go back home and put the covers over my head. This occurred as I experienced the anxiety but it continued to place one foot in front of the other.

When I think back, the behavioral modification technique was similar to what my parents taught us. Specifically, I was told to hold my head up high, walk with my shoulders stretched back, and walk like I know where I was going. In other words, fake it until you make it. On that note, my mother always said, " One thing I admire about you is your strength to go get help if you need it." I never really understood her admiration until days like today. I would inquire from the medical community regarding my condition. In retrospect, that is an admirable trait, as many still suffer in silence.

The night I wrote this, I set a goal to take a shower and groom for five consecutive days. So, one might say, that is no feat. However, when a person is suffering from an illness and struggles to show self-love, my friend… it's a feat. Keeping in mind that glorified birdbaths do not count, I had to learn to appropriately show love by taking care of myself.

A major part of the turnaround for me in my life was acknowledging who I was and who I wasn't. I am a child of the Most High God with inherited benefits. I was a phenomenal woman right then. I was good enough. I had all I needed within me.

I finally began loving myself for real at 40. It was not until 50 that I totally accepted myself; the good, the bad, and the courageous. I learned that self-love or healthy self-esteem is an evaluation, and acceptance is an attitude. So, I was in evaluation mode for ten more years. I must admit that I did have a change in my attitude at 50! I loved it, and I knew it was happening. I walked differently; I had developed a high pep in my step! My thought pattern was elevated. I wore it well and continue to do so.

To you truly love and accept the person you are, you must overcome negative and critical self-talk. Indeed, we can often be our own worse critics. While self-evaluation is a good thing, being overly critical or not identifying what you love about yourself will leave you discovering later in life what could have been discovered sooner.

So, how do you overcome negative, overly critical thinking patterns? I have included some exercises that will put you on the path to reconstructing your life as it pertains to how you think of yourself.

Identifying Self-Critical Talk Exercise:

We all have common phrases that we often speak to ourselves. Are there specific core phrases that you tend to say to yourself? How does that negative voice sound?

Negative Things I Say About Myself:

_____

_____

_____

_____
_____

Positive Replacements:

_____
_____
_____
_____
_____

Identifying Core Beliefs and Their Roots

You have identified the negative, self-critical talks that you say to yourself. Now, you must identify the root of those negative words and beliefs. Was it because a parent said… or a teacher said… or was there a specific event that formed an unhealthy belief about yourself? Think back, and whatever it may be, list it here:

_____
_____
_____
_____
_____

SHOW LOVE NOW:

When showing love now to yourself:

- Take longer luxurious showers and baths with fragrant oils and gels
- Get regular massages
- Eat energizing boosting foods full of fuel for the body
- Exercise to enhance agility and burn fat
- Spiritually feed your soul with the Word of God
- Read affirmations aloud in the mirror
- Associate with people that celebrate you as opposed to those who tolerate you
- Stay in a thankful, grateful, and appreciated space in your mind

List the people in your life that are in this category:

_____
_____
_____
_____
_____
_____
_____

SHOW LOVE NOW

_____
_____
_____

CHAPTER TWO

ACTIVE LISTENING

Have you ever been involved in a conversation, and it seems like the person did not listen to anything you've said? One of the biggest hindrances to our ability to show love nowadays is a lack of understanding. When we do not actively listen, we miss an opportunity to understand the other party's viewpoint.

According to verywellmind.com, active listening refers to a listening pattern that keeps you positively engaged with your conversation partner. It is the process of listening attentively while someone else speaks, paraphrasing and reflecting on what was said and withholding judgment and advice.

Actively listening and speaking the truth to one another in an affectionate manner are the makings of a loving, and very productive relationship; as iron sharpens iron. Well, this is certainly the case for my two comrades. We initially united on a prayer call that met daily, from Monday through Friday. One was my very first sister-in-law, and the other was a church friend and mutual counselor. Individually, each of them had a forty-year and thirty-year-old relationship with me., respectively.

We have a monthly date when we conversed from 6:00 am – 8:00 am on Saturdays. Sometimes our conversations are longer and other times shorter. Still, one thing can be certain, we will address very touchy issues prevalent in each other's lives on every call. I love our authentic interaction. We tend to jump right in with how the month went, what we could have done differently, and our current goals. This may not sound intense, but it has turned out to be a mutually refreshing, refining, and perfecting inter-connection between the three of us. We make the time to address physical health and fitness, mental health, business, entrepreneurial efforts, and financially stabilizing topics.

I honor our relationship. These are two of the ladies from out of town that attended my 60th Birthday bash, and they were also a part of my wedding party. Real troopers and soldiers in the "friend world."

Have you been engaging in active listening? If not, here are some tips that will help improve your active listening skills.

Ways to Engage in Active Listening:

1. Pay attention to body language and body cues

Body language can actually speak louder than words. If you are going to be an active listener, you must watch body language. Research says that over 70% of what we communicate is nonverbal. During your next conversation, pay attention to body cues. Is the person moving a certain way? Are they smiling? Are they tapping their foot? These cues will prove useful in your love journey.

2. Make Eye Contact

Have you ever heard the expression, "The eyes are the windows to the soul" Eye contact is an old but relevant active listening strategy. Looking at someone in the eyes is a sign that you not only hear them but are listening to them. During your next conversation, practice making eye contact and note the effectiveness of this practice.

3. Repeat/Paraphrase what has been spoken

Have you ever been in a conversation and the person said, "Are you listening? If so, tell me what I said?" The ability to repeat or paraphrase what has been said allows for more exchange. It makes the conversant more apt to continue to share.

4. Be present in the conversation

Have you ever been in a conversation, but you were thinking about what you will make for dinner or the tasks you have to complete? This is not active listening. I know some of us pride ourselves on the ability to multitask, but when engaged in conversation, our minds should be clear of any distractions.

SHOW LOVE NOW:

- Openly communicate
- Be honest and loving in your delivery
- Acknowledge the other person's assets and qualities in the conversation
- Give strengths and weaknesses with a positive resolution

List the people in your life that are in this category:

_____
_____
_____
_____
_____
_____
_____

CHAPTER THREE

SICKNESS

There is an ugly monster that has been plaguing our society. It is known as depression. I assume, like most people, when you saw the word "sickness," you thought, " How does this relate?" Usually, when one thinks of illness in our society, the thought is generally related to a "physical" ailment. This chapter will instead address one of the hidden disabilities and illnesses often left unaddressed by many individuals. One of these types of illnesses, as stated earlier, is depression. An exceptionally debilitating disorder, frequently misinterpreted, misunderstood, and greatly undermined by those who never experienced chronic or clinical depression. I am not referring to a bad hair day or morning argument with a significant other. I am specifically talking about the frame of mind that does not rationally decipher reality versus the delusional thoughts of hopelessness.

I experienced depression and observed the difficult journey of depression in a person's life through the demise of my eldest brother.

As it relates to my observation of depression, I can recall my beloved brother comparing himself to his younger siblings during his high school years. While comparing is never the recommended road to take when doing a self-evaluation, often, humans take that route to build honest self-reflection.

My brother was no different. He compared his scholarly abilities to his siblings and other students in his close circle. He was the first sibling of four to graduate from the prestigious Historically Black Colleges and Universities Florida Agricultural and Mechanical University. While he successfully completed his degree, he was saddened because he did so in five years instead of the stipulated four years. Our family was very proud of his accomplishment. However, none of us were in his skin—nor his mind, where all the private and personal turmoil took place.

Before my brother's death at the tender age of 51, he managed to accomplish a bachelor's degree, an honorable discharge from the Army, and was gainfully employed. He enjoyed a loving and caring relationship with the love of his life and fiancé. He also managed to start the process of purchasing a home for his growing family. When

I think of the awesome accomplishments he achieved, I never recalled personally ever making the time to verbalize how proud I was of all he had done in his life. Saddened by this thought, I believe that his life could have ended differently and much later. The mere fact that he did all of this without professional counseling, medication, and the lack of consistent love and encouraging family support was a phenomenal achievement.

Coping With Depression

1. Identify your support system

Depression has a way of making others feel lonely. It can be a tricky disease because it tells the host to do the very opposite of what should be done. It says isolate instead of congregating. It is important to identify and then communicate your expectations for them as a part of your support system.

2. Identifying and Controlling Stressors

Stress is a natural reaction. We were created with a natural built-in fight and flight response. This response system is very helpful in times of trouble. However, too much stress or remaining in a state of stress can cause severe emotional and physical issues. These issues can lead to depression.

3. **Sleep Patterns**

Studies have proven that improper or lack of sleeping patterns can cause many disturbances in the body. It is recommended that each person gets a minimum of 8 hours of sleep per night. While sleep disturbances do not cause depression, they can further facilitate it. Practice getting at minimum, 6-8 hours of sleep per night.

4. **Seeking Counseling**

Counseling can be a great coping mechanism or tool to help address depression. Suppose you can locate a licensed therapist to express life and life circumstances. In that case, it may help in loving oneself and others who deal with depression.

SHOW LOVE NOW:

When encouraging a person during any sickness:

- Send a quick text, for instance; " Thinking of you, with healing thoughts."
- Send an email that includes your recollection of the challenges they experienced in the past and overcame and your hopefulness of their full recovery
- Send a get-well card online to their email

- Send a card to their home or office address (it is nice to receive mail that isn't a bill)
- Take a meal or have dinner delivered to them

List the people in your life that are in this category:

(Family, people in civic, religious, and Greek organizations, co-workers)

_____
_____
_____
_____
_____
_____
_____
_____
_____

CHAPTER FOUR

DEPRESSION/SUICIDE

Depression was a regular, and frequent struggle in my life as far as I can remember from approximately seven years old. I remember as a young adult in my twenties reviewing childhood pictures. I frequently commented that I was a sad-looking child. The facial expressions were dull, the eyes were far away from the actual camera and photographer. I was 28 years old before it was brought to my attention of a very serious abusive occurrence. I was advised by a relative that I had been physically assaulted with a stick to my right shoulder, resulting in a broken collar bone and paralysis on the entire right side of my body. It turns out that at seven years old, I had been extremely sad and very depressed. This disposition was a direct result of the physical abuse I endured but did not report. The actual incident required a four-hour surgery to remove the broken rib that abruptly pressured on a nerve. Then the rehabilitation to re-learn to walk and regain strength in my entire right side was lengthy. This was the beginning of a life of both verbal and physical abuse. Fast-forwarding to my teenage years, I befriended a young woman who was also new to the community. While she said some very horrible and insulting words to me, I thought that was where the abuse ended. It was not enough to insult me verbally; she further lied to her boyfriend that I was secretly attracted to him.

She claimed that I wanted to be intimate with him but that I would never verbalize that to him. So, the abuse continued with aggravated attempted rape. Fast-forwarding to my freshman year in college. More intimidating friendships and actual rapes. All of this was quite emotionally debilitating. After many continued bouts with depression, I managed to enter another intimidating, verbally and physically abusive relationship and marriage. To date, the most humiliating experience that occurred was the "kick to my abdomen," to the tune of the loss of what would have been my second child. This contributed to more stress and depression. The abuse from childhood opened the door to the acceptance of more similar treatment. After eight years of subjecting myself to this unacceptable behavior, I found the courage to walk away.

Another marriage 25+ years later resulted in more abuse. This time emotionally, financially, and through social abuse and neglect. After ending this relationship seven years later. I somehow felt the need to try marriage again with the same individual; until I realized 90 days into the remarriage that nothing had changed or would change. This time on Valentine's Day, the relationship ended finally in divorce again. Sickness, as I discovered, is not exclusively physical. Illness can occur in both the mind and the heart. After five-plus decades of being mistreated and attempting to cover the hurt and pain with an emotionally feel-good pill and/or some other substitute. I had hoped to mask my true agony of depression and subconsciously justify five suicidal ideation experiences. I stopped, got off the emotionally exhausting runaway train, and sought true healing, resolution, and restoration from the true and living God. I resolved that I would live and not die but declare the works of the Lord. (Psalm 118:17) I also had some exceptional talk and art therapists that walked me through some very tough memories.

As it relates to my friendships, who could, I really trust to share this with and not be judged harshly or feel embarrassed? There was a total of five women I could confide in throughout the fifty-year ordeal. I confided in these women at different times, and I felt safe to be ruthlessly honest. Fortunately, I always invested in a great therapist.

Only twice in fifty years did I have a therapist I was uncomfortable being totally honest with. The friendships I was blessed to experience walked with me through academic hardships, domestic violence, miscarriages, mental hospitalizations, career challenges, three marriages, weight loss, weight gain, death of family members, successful accomplishments, and an array of things that I no longer remember. According to research, generally, people challenged with clinical depression have difficulty maintaining relationships. My ability to maintain long-term relationships with friends and family came from my tenacity and focus on becoming strong. Today, I am very proud of the relationships that I have maintained, as they are authentic and mutually beneficial.

Suicide

Trauma is real and can have a lasting impact on the lives of all parties involved. If you are facing some form of trauma, please seek professional counseling or other avenues to address and heal from the traumatic event(s).

Please note, if you or a loved one is currently having thoughts of suicide, which are thoughts of hurting yourself or having thoughts to hurt others, please STOP and contact the national

suicide prevention hotline at **1-800-273-8255. They are available 24/7.**

SHOW LOVE NOW:

When showing love to people facing trauma and other challenging experiences:

- Peruse and share SAVE.org; a website addressing suicide and depression
- Be kindhearted, sensitive when speaking
- Develop great listening skills
- Be supportive, encouraging, and reminding them of other successful feats
- Bring or send flowers (it brightens their space)
- Encourage them to have a meal or coffee with you
- Send "thinking of you" cards (See chapter 9 of Show Love Now)
- Write a short note outlining the great things you recall of their life.

List the people in your life that are in this category:

_____

_____

SHOW LOVE NOW

CHAPTER FIVE

MY DREAM GUY

There are so many broken homes in our world today. Many homes are absent of fathers, and this desperately needs to change. Too often than not, daughters formulate their idea of what the dream guy looks like from their perspective and understanding of their father. Without the father's representation in many homes, daughters can formulate their dream guys from television and popular culture. This formation may not be the best because the culture is fickle, changing, and fleeting. I believe this is one reason for the high divorce rate in many nations.

My daddy was my dream guy. His overall style was fun, loving, even-tempered, happy, and hopeful. I have fond memories as far back as three years old with him. I would sit on his lap, and he would bounce me on his knee. I was the third of four children and the first princess in the bunch. My mother used to say how happy they were to finally get their first female child.

I remember my father coming in from work excited to see us, showering, and meeting us for dinner at 6:30 pm daily. In retrospect, it was so comforting to have our dad with us at the dinner table and his deep voice asking questions about our day in school.

I recall that on the weekends, my dad would periodically take us to Coney Island. He would get on the rides with us, laughing all the way. I remember one occasion getting on the Himalayas, a ride that took you around and around in a circle at full speed. He said, " That will be my last time on that ride." I realize at that point he was getting older, and all that going around in circles caused too much dizziness for him. Dad still allowed us to enjoy the rides, though.

In my high school years, my dad was very instrumental in my life. Dad taught me to drive in his truck. It was so much fun, hearing him yell, " Slow down, put on your signal light, watch the driver in front of you, put on your brakes." Then he was the sergeant figure, as I attempted dating. That did not always work out well, as we could not reach common ground on the guys I liked and the guys he preferred for me. It was okay; I later went off to college in another state. While he was a loving father, he was not lacking in disciplining us as well. The one and only time I recall getting on his bad side and feeling his wrath was when he sent me on a time-sensitive errand. I was asked to go and pick up his paycheck at around noon. Well, I was so glad to have the car, I took a joy ride right over to the college campus. As I lost track of time, I looked up, and it was 4:00 pm when I finally arrived home with the check. My father was waiting at the door. My eyes were as large as teacups. I never recall a look like that on his face toward me. He said, " Where were you? I have been waiting for you for hours. It does not take that long to get there and back. Now the bank is closed. Go to your room!" I did not understand the big deal that day. However, as an adult trying to run a household, paying bills, and so forth, not having access to funds from a Friday to Monday can be a hardship. Of course, I apologized repeatedly, but it did not change the reality of the bank closing.

Moving right along, when I finally did graduate (10 years after high school, so keep pressing if that is your goal), My dad was so proud and happy for me. Over the years, we lived a great distance away from one another. He and my mother visited all of us throughout the United States. When he was about 79 years old, dad took his final drive to see the "girls." While visiting, he became incapacitated because of the onset of a debilitating illness. It was then that the family permanently moved our parents closer to the girls. For exactly one year, I was privileged to live in the same space as my daddy. It was such a precious time. Each day my dad would be so happy. I would see him still getting on his knees by his bedside to pray. That brought back the sweetest memories; I remember him kneeling by his bedside all my life. Today, I wonder what his prayer would be for me? Despite his health condition, he was still grateful, hopeful, and a happy camper. I remember how ecstatic he was to vote for and see Senator Barack Obama become the 44th President and the first African American President of America. Every time dad would hear certain military music being played, he would salute.

My last Thanksgiving dinner with my dad and mom was quite memorable for several reasons. Traditionally, my family celebrates the holiday together at Thanksgiving. For many years, my three siblings and I would travel near and far to come home to my dad's potato salad and mom's macaroni and cheese. This Thanksgiving was significantly different because my dad was present; unfortunately, he could not eat cooked food. Instead of enjoying delicious foods, he was on a complete liquid diet through what is referred to as a "P.E.G." (percutaneous endoscopic gastrostomy). What a difficult time for my dad and a challenging time for our family to observe him in this condition. More specifically, while we were in the dining room, my dad was seated in his favorite recliner in the family room, observing us as we ate. While he knew he had an apparatus in his abdomen, he could not connect to why he could not have dinner with us. We waited hours to eat in hopes that dad would fall asleep during a short nap. Not so. Instead, once we finally sat down to eat, he would periodically ask, " Can I taste the candied yams?" Sadly, one of us would say not right now, dad. My mom would periodically bring over some apple sauce for him to taste. To no avail, dad would circle back around to ask again, " Can I taste the candied yams?"

What a frustrating moment for us all; we ended dinner early that year.

He died approximately six months later. That was such a challenging moment for this daddy's girl. I assisted my mom with all the details of the arrangements. I was scheduled to speak at the service, but I was so broken that I do not recall speaking on the day of the service. I remember doing the closing of the casket finalities, putting the cover over his face, and helping the undertaker close the casket. It was great having no regrets.

Showing love is about valuing relationships, but it is also about restoring relationships. If you have a father, I encourage you to seek forgiveness and restoration. The value and importance of a father have often been diminished, but he is needed. There is no need to live with regrets; if possible, restore the relationship today.

SHOW LOVE NOW:

While your parents, grandparents, aunts, uncles, and cousins are still alive, take the time to show love now.

- Schedule a specific time to reach out on your phone:
- Schedule time to visit
- Set the frequency of calls and limit the amount of time on the call if necessary
- Text messages and pictures
- Send cards [thinking of you] (see additional ideas from Chapter 9)
- Send flowers
- Gift cards (a restaurant, their favorite department store or boutique, grocery store if they are avid bakers and cooks)

_____
_____
_____
_____
_____
_____
_____
_____

CHAPTER SIX

COURTSHIP-WEDDING-MARRIAGE

I was asked to assist a fellow brother in the gospel with planning his beloved wife's home-going services. The task was familiar to me, as two weeks prior, I planned the funeral service for a close friend's mother. Details of the "how-to" were back in my mind. I cautiously made the initial phone call to the brother to assess where I needed to begin. To my surprise, the bereaved brother's initial need was to continue removing articles from his home as the couple was in the process of relocating. Secondly, his request was to have his home cleaned. My immediate thoughts were to find someone he could trust to come into his vulnerable space and someone who could effectively and efficiently complete the assigned job. I was currently utilizing a girlfriend to clean my home. I also needed some muscle to move items as well as to clean. My ex-husband was the ideal candidate. I pitched my ideas to the brother and identified how I knew them both. I trusted them to team up and get the job done. The brother gladly agreed and accepted my suggestion. The next order of business was compiling information for the obituary and the order of service. His sister-in-law was on hand to assist with the names of the family members for the obituary. While in the background, the cleanup process continued.

Unbeknown to me (which I later found out), he questioned my ex-husband about how he could let me get away? I am told that my ex-husband responded that he was not ready for a serious relationship. On the second day, he reiterated the question to my ex-husband. This time, the response was his addiction got in the way. In the days following, he asked me why I wouldn't reconcile with my ex-husband, who obviously still loved me? I replied quite bluntly, " Did he mention that I married him twice?" He was taken aback, then he smiled and said, "No, actually, he didn't mention that." I continued by reiterating that "I am done; stick a fork in it!" His facial expression was somehow one of relief. Throughout this line of inquiry, I resolved that this brother and pastor was doing his due diligence to assist in the decline of Christian divorce by gently counseling and guiding.

Throughout the planning of his deceased wife's service, I had no indication that this grief-stricken individual was remotely interested in or desirous of another relationship. One day, after finalizing the funeral details, and completing the tasks at hand, I went overtime. I was scheduled to be at work within two hours and had not eaten or returned the brother to his home. In a very caring and concerned manner, he asked if we could go to lunch together? Continuing, he said I would like to do that for your tireless assistance to me. I replied yes; he asked where I would like to go? I said I am not very picky; what do you like to eat? He replied seafood. So, I asked, "A local seafood restaurant or a national seafood restaurant?" He preferred the latter, and we agreed. So, we arrived at the restaurant, and while eating lunch, out of nowhere, he asked, "How old are you?" I said, "How old do you think I am?" He casually said "52." I smiled and said, "Really, no but thank you, I am60." He casually stated, "My first wife was 10 years older than me." I chuckled and said, "Okay." As I looked at the menu. The waiter asked if we were ready to order? He was ready, and he knew what he wanted. So, I quickly made a choice, and I noticed him smiling at me from across the table. I said, " So, what's so funny?" He said, "I was thinking how you do not look your age. You come across much younger." I replied, "Thank you," with a smile. After lunch, I dropped him off and went to work.

While at work, he came by to review the initial draft of the obituary and program. He took it home to read and asked if we could meet when I got off work. Well, after my shift, we met up. I thought our meeting would be to make corrections and required changes. However, he asked if he could date me exclusively. I asked, "Date me exclusively? What is that? Do you mean like grade school when one would write a note do you like me check the box yes or no?" He laughed and said, "Yes, just like that." I said, "Well, yes, I can do that." I was dumbfounded! "What have I done?" I was totally blindsided. Then what do you know, we had a tremendous number of things in common and were married thirty days later. Life with him is blissful! Ninety days later, we had a beautiful wedding on my parent's anniversary, which is the day after Valentine's Day.

WEDDING

When my husband learned that I never had a wedding, he insisted that I began planning. A dream wedding is what it was indeed. I remember planning my wedding in a home economics class at 16 years old. Of course, I have updated the plan a few times since then.

I was excited about our wedding date being my parent's 58th marriage anniversary. I was elated at the color scheme surrounding Valentine's Day. Red, white, and silver accents were the color scheme. The bridal attendants wore my favorite color: Candy apple red! We located beautiful red gowns. The men in attendance wore light gray suits similar in color to silver.

In addition to the bridal attendants above, I wanted some very special ladies dressed in silver. The silver ladies (as they were lovingly referred to) were my many friends who walked with me through different points in my life. After going through my list of ladies that dated back to 1980, I asked many, of whom the majority were unavailable to be a part of my wedding. Amongst those who were available, I was honored to have my childhood friend, a prayer partner, my active listening partner, a former co-worker, a longtime friend, and the woman who invited me to the church where I met my husband.

These beautiful attendants wore beautiful silver knee-length dresses of their choice. Their primary responsibility was to individually give me the flowers that made up my bouquet. As I walked down the aisle, I would receive a few flowers from each lady, hug them, and thank them for their many years of love and for being at my wedding.

Then I chose my music, my live vocalist, and the pianist team. The D.J. and two planners who assisted greatly with the details of the day were also friends. The white chair covers and red sashes, to the red and white plates and chargers, the red roses all over the room as centerpieces, rose boutonnieres, and bouquets. Everything was so beautiful and carefully thought out. The caterer, photographer, videographers, dancer, and guests at the wedding were all so very beautiful. I was so pleasantly surprised when I entered the room. As I walked down the aisle, I saw my dear pastors, and my eyes were fixated on my handsome groom. Oh, what a glorious day!

MARRIAGE

Eight months into our dream marriage, I mapped out a Wednesday as "His Day." After shopping for items that day, I arrived home rather late. So, I ensured that he was comfortable in the prayer room; I then took a warm shower. I remembered that I did not pick up a greeting card like we both frequently did. So, the idea to be a human greeting card came to me. After the luxurious shower, I took red lipstick and placed the letter "I" on my right breast, sketched a "heart" on the left breast, and a "U" on the middle of my stomach, spelling I love you. I took the yellow and white ribbon, wrapped it around my neck and shoulders, and then brought the ribbon through my arms to tie a beautiful bow upon my stomach. I softly spoke out, "Hun, this is your day; I first want you to read your card." Immediately, I stepped around the corner in my enhanced birthday suit. His face lit up like a

Christmas tree. After we went through the card, I shared his second gift, a case of his favorite soft drink. He smiled at the thoughtfulness.

Gift three was brought in; A 50-bag case of his favorite popcorn! He was all smiling. For the fourth gift, I brought in a beautifully crocheted cell phone carrier (Moments before he commented on mine). The fifth gift was two dozen long yellow and red stem roses. He buried his head in the bulbs capturing the fragrance. Still smiling and laughing, he said thank you so much; no one has ever done this for me. I said, hold up, wait for a minute, Hun, for the culmination. I came prancing around the corner with gift six, a beautiful small black shopping bag. He said, " That's a jewelry store bag." I said, " Oh really?" He chuckled as he quickly and excitedly removed the wrapped box from the bag. He kept staring at me, smiling as he continued opening the box. Finally, he pulled his gift out of the bag and pulled off the wrapping paper. He hurriedly opened the box and was flabbergasted at his stunning watch.

He thanked me and reminded me that no one had ever done anything like that for him before. I just smiled, as I was thankful for the gift of a loving friend and phenomenal husband that I had been blessed with by God! We frequently say to each other, "You were worth the wait!" and " This is not that!"

SHOW LOVE NOW:

- Be creative and innovative, do not wait for holidays to show love now
- Make a personalized gift
- Give or mail a greeting card
- Make the time to send a special "I appreciate you" text
- Take the time to compile an email highlighting the fondest memories you are most grateful for
- Plan and execute a memorable "carpet outing"
- Plan and execute a dinner and movie night

Reflect: Think about your journey with your mate/spouse. What are some of the moments in which you were able to show love?

_____
_____
_____
_____
_____
_____
_____
_____

SHOW LOVE NOW

CHAPTER SEVEN

ANNIVERSARIES

What a cherished memory I experience when I recall my parents' celebration of their 58th anniversary, although my siblings and I previously discussed publicly waiting to celebrate their 60th anniversary, which would be a significant time for them both. I specifically remember alerting my siblings that I sensed the need to make a big deal about the 58th anniversary. Our dad had been through a major illness, and quite a bit had transpired within the previous 18 months. My dad had experienced some health challenges surrounding a stroke. Paralysis began to affect his throat; he had frequent bouts with pneumonia.

As a result, my sister and I frequently traveled from Florida to Virginia. Leading up to their anniversary, the following occurred. When our parents visited us in Florida, the diagnosis of aspiration pneumonia was discovered. At that point, the doctors recommended that my dad should not be moved out of the state. That is when our family went into "relocation mode." We literally needed God's grace to sell their home and my home and purchase one home large enough to comfortably house the three of us. Comfortably, implied having my father's hospital bed in the same room as their queen-size bed; they were literally inseparable. They occasionally had "loud fellowship," but the two frequently made fond memories for the greater part of their lives. When the three of us (dad, mom, and I) came together under one roof as adults, the loving memories of their interaction were again revealed to me. This upcoming anniversary would be their last. As my siblings and I prepared for that special day, we ensured that both parents had cards and gifts for one another.

Additionally, we purchased an array of significant engraved gifts for them. We decorated them in gold (for year 50 and white for year 60). We celebrated with a festive dinner, with gifts and poetry during the surprise tribute. This eventful evening was certainly a warm and fuzzy experience. As they went down memory lane. My parents individually shared so many extraordinary times. They recalled meaningful moments through their time together. Much later, when Dad passed on, retrospectively, it all made sense why we needed to focus on celebrating their relationship two years early. My "Dream Guy," who was a loving father, dependable provider, and strong statured man, daddy would die nine months later.

Anniversary Game Activities

1. Read the book "The 5 Love Languages" by Gary Chapman and take the quiz!

This is an interactive and fun way to learn more about your spouse and how they receive love. It is important to identify your spouse or future spouse's love language to ensure you speak their language. This way, both parties are filled with love!

2. How Well Do You Know Your Spouse?

In this activity, each spouse answers questions about the other spouse on a sheet of paper. At the end of the timer, the couple reveals their answer simultaneously. This is another way to have fun with your spouse and learn more about them.

3. Memory Lane

In this activity, the couple will take some time to stroll down memory lane. The couple will answer questions about... When was your first kiss? What was your first happy memory together? When and to what song was your first dance? When did you know that you were in love?

SHOW LOVE NOW:

- Add the anniversary of significant individuals to your phone
- Send a card that includes a restaurant gift card
- Take or send a fruit basket
- Call on the day and extend your loving greeting
- Plan a celebratory event

List the people in your life that are in this category:

_____

_____

_____

_____

_____

_____

_____

_____

_____

_____

CHAPTER EIGHT

EMPLOYMENT

When it came to a career, it was most challenging to maintain a position for any considerable length of time. Interestingly, the longest I maintained one job was three years, mainly because it was my favorite job. This position occurred as I was completing my Master's degree in Social Work. So, after being hired and working for a year, I inquired about utilizing my internship position, and it was granted. Working on a job, in general, was not a difficult task. However, after the 12 months elapsed, I felt like I did average when my evaluation came up for review. This was discouraging to me. Then, the new expectations and standards came into play. I personalized these actions by interpreting them as I was being picked on or singled out.

As a direct result of some medication reactions, I would occasionally have what seemed like a hangover. This caused me to oversleep and often clocked in late. The very nature of my depression disorder would encompass days when I was unable to attend work, and when I could attend work, it was sometimes difficult to focus and or concentrate on the assignment at hand. Thus, causing anxiety and aiding in my inability to efficiently do my job. This combination of challenges frequently reiterated my feeling of being inadequate and ultimately strengthened the conviction that I was a failure. Looking back, I should have used my disability to have certain accommodations documented for me.

This illness and lack of job consistency negatively affected my finances. The inconsistent diet of fast foods often left me lacking the cash in my budget to pay all my bills. The fact that I could not make it to work on time and frequent absences from work drastically reduced my pay. These factors further justified my self-loathing feelings of low self-esteem and feelings of failure.

Often, when we experience co-workers or subordinates who appear to underachieve, these are indications that an underlying problem may be occurring. Rather than write them off as lazy or not a team player, kindly inquire further. Other common hidden disabilities come to mind. A few include diabetes, fibromyalgia, arthritis, and migraines. People are generally fearful of being forthcoming with their disabilities for fear of losing their job or not getting hired for the job. This is food for thought. As I continue with this chapter, keep in mind that many people work from home due to the pandemic. A high percentage of employers were exposed to the fact they are receiving a higher incidence of productivity. If I had been able to work from home during some of my challenging times, I would have been effective in my work also.

So, a great time to show love now is during a person's career moves and advancements. Specifically, when a person obtains a position, particularly after a lengthy period of unemployment. It is admirable and fitting to acknowledge the person's accomplishment. It is kind and encouraging to support the person in this way.

Another opportunity to acknowledge the accomplishments of others occurs when the individual receives a much-desired promotion. An acknowledgment of this occasion is a great time to show love now and support that individual. This indicates that people often wish and hope others notice their work, so this is a great opportunity to express that you notice and are proud of their accomplishments. The businesswoman Mary Kay Ash said that everyone has an invisible sign hanging from their neck saying, "Make me feel important." Furthermore, people should never forget this message when working with people.

Another very special time of acknowledgment is retirement. When one has completed their career journey and then transitions to a new mission in their life, it is commendable to recognize this momentous milestone.

When I think of these very special occurrences, my aunt's retirement celebration comes to mind. There were well over two hundred guests in the room. As the pianist played classical music, the room was beautifully decorated. The dais table was set with an array of dignitaries. My uncle escorted my aunt into the room as the excitement from the mass of guests roared in appreciation and pride. The Master of ceremony preceded to announce the incoming of the honoree. The wind beneath my wings played as the soloist sang the words so lovingly to the honoree. After a lengthy standing ovation, the Master of ceremony acknowledged my aunt. He began the list of accomplishments, accolades, and acknowledgments. Following, one by one, the guest speakers enthusiastically spoke of their relationship and experiences with the honoree. Each speaker elaborated on the impact she had on her family, employment, the community, and the political arena.

In between the speakers were songs, poems, and a delicious dinner. The evening continued in a historical manner. Then finally, it was time to hear from the honoree. She stood up teary-eyed from ingesting all the beautiful observations from her family, co-workers, supervisors, neighbors, and community leaders. The beautiful acknowledgments given to her by the guest speakers were so impactful. Then she received a showering of flowers, an array of gifts, donations in her name to the non-profit of her choice, and a vehicle from her husband. This event was so powerful.

Being present as a guest was a great feeling and an experiential way to show love now. It was supportive and admirable, as we acknowledged the pride we possessed for the honoree.

Employers

Employers must understand the importance of showing love to their employees who may face various situations while being employed. Managers should engage employees, not to invade or overstep the personal-professional boundary but to ensure employees feel safe at work. Research has shown that employees who feel that their employers care about them and what happens in their personal lives are more apt to have lower turnover rates than those who show no regard for their employees.

Employers must implement sensitivity training but more so a love model. This love model will show employees that they are more than hired help; they are like family. A good suggestion is to have monthly "care" meetings. These meetings allow the managers to interact with employees and their families. These events produce relationships and mutual bonds. People are more apt to take an interest when they know or are acquainted with the parties.

SHOW LOVE NOW:

When acknowledging a person's new job, a promotion, or a retirement:

- Send a quick congratulatory acknowledgment on a social media platform
- Send an email that includes your recollection of the challenges they experienced
- Send a card online to their email
- Send a card to their home or office address (it is nice to receive mail that is not a bill)

List the ways that you can show love in the workplace:

_____
_____
_____
_____
_____
_____
_____
_____
_____

CHAPTER NINE

FUNERALS

When I think of funerals, one funeral that stands out in my mind, and that was the funeral service for my beloved former father-in-law, whom I will refer to as dad. A prolific speaker, teacher, and an exceptional family man, dad was a phenomenal individual. During the celebration of his life, there was standing room only in a considerably large New York City Church. The celebratory program listed dignitaries, co-laborers in the gospel, and families that spoke of their memories and impact on the beloved pastor's life. When I think about the number of people who showed up for this gathering versus the people who contacted him during his very lengthy illness, I am sadly disappointed. The crux of my disappointment stemmed from the fact that within his lifetime, many of the people that celebrated my dad in his death did not actively celebrate him during his life. Dad (as I referred to him) always enjoyed hearing my voice when I phoned him from Florida. The inflection in his voice was cheerful and warm. A year could pass, and I would be sure to call him for his birthday. He was thrilled that I thought of him and actually followed up on that thought with a phone conversation. There were occasions when I would send a "Thinking of you" card. In either case, reaching out to dad always had an encouraging effect on him. It would warm my heart and encourage me to continue showing love now to him and others. An "encouraging effect," you might say? Those few moments caused him to go a little further in his "press and determination" to stay alive. In retrospect, what if all the dignitaries, co-laborers in the gospel, family members, and loved ones, near and far, each reached out to him during the 365 days? Would he have held on just a little longer in this life as a direct result of individuals celebrating his presence? No, I cannot prove that indeed he would have lived longer had this occurred. Yet, I certainly can prove that the interaction I received from family, friends, associates, and acquaintances certainly preserved my life when I was extremely down with severe depressive episodes. As the upbeat, and optimistic person dad was, I am almost certain that regular stimulation from interactions with each of the well-wishers that attended the homegoing celebration would have indeed encouraged his longevity.

Good vibes stimulate the mind, reduce blood pressure, and can extend life for people. Further, in the *Medical News Today* article, dated July 28, 2010, Dr. Catherine Paddock stated that "Low social interaction harms Lifespan on a Par with obesity, smoking, and inactivity."

The need for stimulation and social interaction is particularly great for seniors; those struggling with illnesses and related experiences. Divorce, loss of a job, and death of a child or other loved ones are a few experiences that negatively affect the psyche.

Initially, people respond during a crisis, but there is often no long-term consistency. I would recommend when the onset of a challenge occurs, it is great to initially respond with an acknowledgment, but a follow-up is encouraging. Follow-up is essential; after the initial incident, the crowd of well-wishers go back to their affairs, and are the victims left alone in the situation.

Waste no time! Tell those that mean a lot to you how much you value them. How much you love them and how much they are needed. Can you practice showing love today? Maybe you know someone, a friend, a co-worker who has lost a loved one. During times of difficulty, a caring call from a friend can make all the difference.

There is one aspect that we have not addressed in regards to funerals. Another way to show love is to prepare your final wishes for those that you love. Death, in and of itself, is difficult. When loved ones have to make decisions that they are unsure you would support, it causes further grief and uncertainties if they made a choice that the deceased is happy with. Discuss with your family/friends to ensure your final wishes are known, or write your wishes down and put them in a place where your loved ones can access them. A good document that can help with wishes is called "5 Wishes". The "5 Wishes" document can be found at www.5wishes.org. I must note that I am not affiliated with this organization and can only offer this website as a resource if needed.

SHOW LOVE NOW:

When sending condolences:

- Send a card to their home or office address (it is nice to receive mail that is not a bill)
- Send flowers/ plants or a donation to their favorite charity
- Send an email that includes your recollection of the wonderful memories of the person
- Send a card online to their email
- Wait a week or ten days out after the funeral/cremation services to reach out via telephone or any of the above suggestions.

(After the initial fanfare, the family is sadly left alone without their loved one.)

List the people in your life that are in this category:

_____

_____

_____

_____

_____

_____

_____

_____

_____

CHAPTER TEN

BIRTHDAYS

I celebrated my 60th birthday. This was a very important day for me. As I read in the scripture, "Genesis 6:3," we could realistically reach 120 years old; That would put me halfway to that point. I wanted to rejoice with those in my immediate circle. I was born and raised in Brooklyn, New York. I completed two years of high school in Virginia and graduated college in Florida. As a direct result of residing in multiple states. I had a plethora of acquaintances throughout the country. When I began to construct my birthday celebration list, the names that came to mind were individuals that resided in various cities.

When I requested an individual to attend my celebration, I can recall getting a little push back from my out-of-town guests. I sensed because the event was on a Saturday morning, those who would have to fly in would have to consider coming into my city on Friday evening. Then they would have to obtain lodging, food, and ground transportation.

I viewed attaining 60 years of age as a significant lifelong achievement. So, I wanted to share this moment with individuals with whom I encountered so many memories. I was a little taken aback by the resistance. So, when I approached the next set of out-of-town guests, I stated, in the beginning, the following, "if I passed away, you would probably travel here to attend my service, yes?" They would reply, where are you going with this? I would then continue by stating, "I would not know you were present at the memorial service." Further, "I am having my 60th birthday celebration, and it would really mean a lot if you would consider attending the celebration and forfeit my funeral."

To make a very long story short, I recall only two out-of-town guests showing up amongst the twenty people who ultimately attended. I was extremely pleased with the outcome, as the individuals that attended created such a warm, and intimate time of celebration for me. I sincerely sensed that those who were there were the people who were predestined to be there. To that end, I encourage people to share their love for their friends and family on their birthdays while they have the opportunity.

Some people do not want to celebrate with others. They may have had trauma during their childhood and other periods of their lives; that may have caused them not to desire a celebration. While this does occur, you can be the catalyst that aids in creating new memories and beginning a tradition of celebrating their restructuring thought patterns. Often in the cognitive restructuring theory, old thoughts do transcend into new realities. This occurs when one replaces a thought or memory with a newly conceived concept. The result is that the replaced thought, and memory resounds, and with repetition, it overlays the old thought and becomes the new and "current" thought. Ultimately creating a paradigm switch in the person's thought processes.

After sharing with an acquaintance about this chapter's contents, I learned that she does not celebrate her birthday. I shared with her the ideal ways of creating new memories. Her reply was astonishing to me, as she did not want to recreate new memories. Even though I thought that was sad, I realized the reality of the statement was something I initially heard in my twenties. This may sound callous, but there is great truth in the statement. So here goes, "Some will, some won't, so what."

On the one hand, some people will embrace a thought, others will not. So, kick the dust off your feet and recognize the "So what." Sometimes, I have been disappointed that a person in my counseling days chose not to receive a particular concept. Today, it is much easier for me to say okay, particularly as I feel the wind on my back to continue my journey to find someone that will say, "Yes, I get it! Help me to cognitively restructure my thoughts and memories."

Cognitive restructuring (C.R.) is a psychotherapeutic process of learning to identify and dispute irrational or maladaptive thoughts, known as cognitive distortions. They can be thoughts of all-or-nothing thinking (splitting), magical thinking, over-generalization, magnification, and emotional reasoning, commonly associated with many mental health disorders as defined in Wikipedia.

Birthdays are big deals to many around the world. However, if your friend or family member chooses not to celebrate or acknowledge birthdays, do not be offended. One of the important aspects of love is meeting people where they are. Love means that one respects their choices. You may not always agree with their choices, and that's okay. Don't allow things that can be trivial to hinder the love in any type of relationship. Remember, we mentioned understanding the love languages. This is not only true for intimate relationships but all relationships.

SHOW LOVE NOW:

When acknowledging a person's birthday:

- Use your phone to save significant birthdays
- Send a card to their home or office address (it is nice to receive mail that is not a bill)
- Send a card online to their email
- Send a quick congratulatory acknowledgment on social media
- Send a warm birthday text
- Send flowers
- Send a gift card
- Send a gift item

List the people in your life that are in this category:

_____
_____
_____
_____
_____
_____

SHOW LOVE NOW

CHAPTER ELEVEN

THINKING OF YOU

"Thinking of you" is just sending any form of communication to let someone know that they are in your thoughts. This is absolutely the highest form of compliment you can offer someone. People are consumed with so many thoughts, responsibilities, and commitments that it is especially refreshing to know that someone cared enough to reach out to them. Since we all have busy and occupied lives, often a lengthy conversation is not feasible. However, a thoughtful text, email, or card is a welcomed thought. Occasionally you will find that thoughtful communication can lead to a face-to-face coffee before work, or it might just be the connection for a morning walk. Whatever it leads to, the connection is great, and the time constraints are in place.

There are times when people go through life's crises, and unselfish communication is like a breath of fresh air to them. The person going through a relationship breakup feels comforted. The individual receiving treatments for an illness feels reassured. The one who just left their home because of financial challenges feels consoled. The person that recently lost a loved one feels supported. A "thinking of you" correspondence is almost always appreciated.

I recall years ago when I was gainfully employed as a primary therapist. While I was conducting a group therapy session with eight clients, I literally left the room in my thoughts. This occurred as I heard the story of a woman who was in an abusive relationship. As she shared the horrifying details of a past occurrence, I recalled myself falling down a flight of stairs. I know I emotionally disconnected and left the room for five minutes minimally. When I checked back in with the group, we had five minutes left to close the group. I closed the group and immediately went to my office. My co-worker/therapist asked me, "What just happened in there"? I responded, " What do you mean"? He said, "You seemed preoccupied at the end of the group." I said, "Oh yes, her account of the abuse was very descriptive, but I am okay. Thanks for checking in". That very same day, I was admitted to the psychiatric hospital for evaluation. The diagnosis was anxiety and depression resulting from repressed memories. I was saddened by the hospitalization. Yet, I knew I was in a stressful mental state. I recall the doctors and therapist speaking with me in a very calm tone to not alarm me. I also recall the therapist slowly addressing the reason for my admission. As time unfolded, the reality that an abusive relationship previously suppressed was now surfacing, and it was time to fully address the issue. This entire process took approximately thirty days. During this time, the "thinking of you" cards flooded into the hospital and my home. Fortunately, the cards and notes did not stop coming. The correspondence came for a minimum of six months. There were enough cards to make two five-inch booklets of memories for myself. I punched two holes in every card and then placed a ribbon to connect the cards into a booklet. This proved to be an asset for me in the coming two to three years. I had such negative thoughts in my mind. At some point I held the premonition that people were seeing me differently now, people do not like me as much as before, and I'm not a good therapist. All of which were not true. After being released from the hospital, I remember seeing a physical therapist who spoke such hope in my life. He would say, "These events in your life will make you a more compassionate therapist. These experiences will cause you to have tenacity with other challenging times you will face. Be encouraged and empowered." Comments and the cards from family, friends, pastors, Sunday school teachers, and other parishioners and clergy leaders kept me going. I strongly feel that when we all take part in this aspect of "showing love now," we will see our associates' predicament change for the better. As I gave the example of sharing hope with a person dealing with an illness, these cards, calls, and meals of love could very well be the turnaround of hopelessness. This could cause the person to live longer, thrive, and be revived. The loving act could prevent a funeral, or at best, delay a funeral.

I know a specific group of people who would benefit from "Thinking of You" correspondence would definitely be seniors in our sphere. Whether they are parents, grandparents, aunts, uncles, teachers, professors, politicians, pastors, and ministers that have impacted our lives. During the downside of the mountain in their lives, they need reassurance that things will be alright. So, a "thinking of you" correspondence is much needed. The truth is…if we make it to these ripe older ages, we too will benefit from a plethora of people reaching out to us. The fact of the matter is that after raising children, cuddling nieces and nephews, praying for people, and advocating for others, we all come to a place where we cease from these labors of love. During these times, it would be nice to hear a thank you or job well done, periodically. I recall a retired city official in the town where I reside saying, "I would love to hear someone just say thank you." They were misty-eyed when the words came from their lips. That was the only reason I visited, to remind them of their outstanding work in the community worldwide.

Thinking of you is one of the kindest gestures that one can display.

SHOW LOVE NOW:

- Send a quick text "thinking of you, with heartfelt thoughts."
- Send an email that includes your recollection of the great experiences and how they overcame and will continue to rise to the occasion
- Send a thinking of you card online to their email
- Send a card to their home or office address (it is nice to receive mail that is not a bill)

List the people in your life that are in this category:

_____
_____
_____
_____
_____
_____
_____

SHOW LOVE NOW

CONCLUSION

As I have discussed throughout this book, love is something that we all need. Love unites us and causes us to grow. I hope that you have a sense of love and are charged with urgency to "Show Love Now." There are many reasons and ways to demonstrate the love you have for family, friends, and employees. It should be noted that we should never take it for granted that people "know" how we feel about them. Then we should consider the various ways to show love to different people. When you gain empathy from this book, you will want to show love now.

NOTES

SHOW LOVE NOW

SHOW LOVE NOW

ABOUT THE AUTHOR

SiTerra Wallace-Walker is a Brooklyn, New York native who currently lives in Tallahassee, Florida. She is a wife, certified life and transformational coach, entrepreneur, author, inspirational speaker, facilitator, ordained minister, and most importantly, a servant! She is pastor beside her husband, Bishop Gregory Walker.

"LOVE28, L.L.C." is the manifestation of an inspirational revelation of SiTerra Wallace-Walker received in 2009. Mrs. Wallace-Walker has experienced layers of negativity, which caused her to become more sensitive to life's basic emotion, love. Having worked as a social worker for the past 25 years, Ms. Wallace-Walker has seen many situations that underscored her passion for redirecting people to love themselves first and then each other.

SiTerra has been commissioned to love and has a passionate heart for people. SiTerra's social work arena experience involved crisis care counseling, life skills facilitation, and advocacy. She currently holds a

Bachelor's degree in Sociology & Criminal Justice and a Master's degree in Social Work. She is seeking her Doctorate in Metaphysics.

Love is a very well-known concept; however, many people do not fully understand how to effectively demonstrate love. Branded with the motto "Let Our Values Emerge," LOVE28 is a movement designed to enhance people's perspective of interpersonal relationships by learning to show love now. This will be accomplished by marketing workshops, retreats, seminars, coaching, and everyday items exclusively with the message of love.

As an entrepreneur, she currently serves as the C.E.O. of LOVE28 Corporation and L28CA (LOVE28 Coaching Academy), a school teaching scholar who "shows love now" to themselves and others as they become a Certified Life Coach. LOVE28 is the primary source of this movement, enhancing the awareness of how to show love now.

www.ingramcontent.com/pod-product-compliance
Lightning Source LLC
Chambersburg PA
CBHW051701090426
42736CB00013B/2477